The World is Beautiful:
Two Years on the Road (Photos)

by
Pete Hendley

Also by Pete Hendley

LCI 85: The Military Career of Lt(jg) Coit Hendley Jr. During the Invasions of North Africa, Italy, and Omaha Beach on D-Day: His Papers and Photos

Hiking the Grand Canyon: The South Kaibab and Bright Angel Trails; Photos and Tips

35mm: From Film to Digital

Self-portrait — India

The World is Beautiful:
Two Years on the Road (Photos)

*****

Pete Hendley

Yewell Street Press
fine art publisher

yewellstreetpress.com

Iowa City, Iowa

The World is Beautiful: Two Years on the Road (Photos)
by
Pete Hendley

Copyright ©2019 by Pete Hendley

All rights reserved. No part of this book may be reproduced or used in any manner without written permission of the copyright owner except for the use of quotations in a book review. For more information, contact: yewellstreetpress.com

FIRST EDITION
hc 978-0-9964993-7-8
pb 978-0-9964993-5-4
ebook 978-0-9964993-3-0

www.yewellstreetpress.com

www.petehendley.com

The photo "Men on Train" was the 2019 Single Image Spotlight Winner for Travel Photography in *Black and White Magazine*, December Issue.

To Laurie

TABLE OF CONTENTS

Introduction: The Painful Beauty of Impermanence — 12

1. Awe — 50
2. Driven over the Edge — 94
3. The Dead are Everywhere — 100
4. Too Far — 150
5. Hog-Tied and Crazy — 164
6. But the Earth is Round — 224
7. Hear Monkeys Holler — 242

Introduction: The Painful Beauty of Impermanence

In 1986, a little more than a year after my father died, I went to the airport with a small carry-on duffle bag and flew away. I was twenty-eight. I had no plan. I just had to go.

The neighbor who cleaned my father's house called when he had found him, and I took a cab across Capitol Hill to see him dead on the couch, TV on, scotch in hand, his head back, his mouth open in a small "o".

We buried him next to my mother, who had died suddenly of a cerebral hemorrhage thirteen years earlier. It felt like the ground beneath me had collapsed.

The world had grown cold to me even before his death. I had been barely hanging on. I hated my job and had lost hope and I had no ideas except the one: to leave.

I first landed in Brussels and then made my way south to Paris, where I took a room near the Eiffel Tower. A neon sign lit my window. I walked around the city for a few days and then caught a train south into Portugal — to Lisbon and then Lagos, a small seaside town where I pulled my back carrying my duffel over one shoulder for so long. I laid in bed for three days until I could get up again then went on into the Sagres region in southwest Portugal, on the ocean. There I met other travelers who talked about the places they had been: Thailand, China, Australia, Tahiti. After a week, I hitched a ride up through Spain with a German guy on his way back to Berlin for his national service in the military. It was a long trip, and to save money we would pull over and sleep by the side of the road at night. In Seville, someone smashed the car window and stole his backpack while we ate at a cafe nearby. They rifled through mine but since I had nothing of value, nothing was taken. The German dropped me off in Milan later at a train station in the middle of the night, and I sat afraid while I tried to figure out where to go next. I decided to make my way south to Greece and find a warm, sunny island. I began taking trains south through Italy, a few hours at a time, stopping in small towns and finding rooms for a night or two or three. Eventually I reached Rome: the Colosseum, the Trevi Fountain. I walked the bustling streets for more than a week, until the urge to keep moving, to do, to just go, pushed me on again.

The days had turned into weeks and the weeks into months: France, Portugal, Spain, Italy. When I finally arrived in Athens, I was too late for the sun and the warmth, and the islands I'd imagined visiting were closed for the winter. Instead, I lingered at the Acropolis and the Parthenon and walked through the noisy markets. I spent days in cafes just sitting. I'd read, write in my journal, take photos, and think about my situation. The weather became even colder and I started thinking about going home. I had been gone four months by then. I felt exhausted and defeated. What I was doing was pointless. Nothing had changed. The world was indeed bleak.

I went to get a ticket home at the chaotic Syntagma Square in the center of Athens. The sun was just starting to peek out from behind the clouds for the first time in days, and I found myself standing in front of a very tall sign that displayed a list of places all over the world—and how much it cost to go to each one. I had never heard of most of them. I discovered that I could buy a ticket to India with a year stopover in Cairo for far less than what a ticket back to Washington D.C. cost. It would actually be cheaper to keep going than to go home. The practicality of it was irresistible to me. I studied the list, and it dawned on me how little I knew of the world. Suddenly, I became aware, in a new way, of the opportunity in front of me. I had to see more.

It would be two years before I would head back home to the States.

So, I went to Cairo. And then I went through the Middle East and into Asia: India, China, Indonesia. Then Australia and beyond.

Those were the days before email and cell phones. Personal computers had just arrived, though few people used them yet. While traveling, I would write letters home and then wait weeks to get one in return. I would wait in line at storefronts to make international phone calls through an operator, the connections scratchy and distant, while the clock ticked away my money. I would tell people which city to write to me in next and then would pick up their letters at the main post office's General Delivery window first thing after arriving.

In Cairo, my camera broke and I asked my older sister to buy me another and ship it to me in Jerusalem. What she sent turned out to be a beautiful stroke of luck—one of the best point-and-shoot film cameras made at the time—a Nikon L35AF2 with its amazingly sharp fixed 35mm f2.8 lens, a camera with a bit of a cult following even all these years later because of that lens.

For years after returning, I didn't look at any of the photos I took because they stirred up a painful ache for things long gone. I missed so many places and people I'd known then, and I missed the rush, the edge, the uncertainty. For a long time, I felt as if something had been lost, though I have had many other adventures since then. I've lived in Mexico and Guatemala, twice hiked to the bottom of the Grand Canyon, and I've been to some of the most beautiful places on earth: Costa Rica, the Cascade Range, the Rockies, Maui, beaches in the Carolinas and Florida. I've seen the Northern Lights from my own backyard in Iowa. I remodeled an old house, started a business, wrote two books, and I fell in love. I have found a measure of peace.

One of the books I wrote is about my two-year trip, and I have included excerpts throughout this book to help explain what was happening around the time these photos were taken.

It all seemed so simple during those years I traveled, once I'd found my way. Just go. Take photographs. Move, do.

There was pain, of course: leaving friends I'd made; waking up confused and alone in Singapore; getting sick in Cairo, India, and Indonesia; enduring claustrophobic two- or three-day train rides in China; driving off the edge of a cliff on a bus in the Himalaya; getting my nose broken in a bar fight in Thailand; watching a shark swim directly toward me on the Great Barrier Reef, sure I would be attacked.

But once I had made the leap that day in front of the tall sign in Athens, I felt as clear as I've ever felt. I was in the right place doing the right thing. During my travels, I remember thinking often: If I die now, it will be ok because this is where I am supposed to be.

Over time, the pain of remembering subsided. Over time, also, digital photography emerged, and a whole new world of editing photos opened up. With the new software, I was able to go back to my old negatives, some thirty years after I had shot them, scan them into a computer, and then really see what I had.

Many of the images I had completely forgotten. Others I remembered as clearly as if I had taken them yesterday. Some were damaged or had faded with age. Others were just bad snapshots. Out of the total of 1700 photographs, the 104 included in this book most captured the world I had seen.

I remember a time when I was traveling when I stood at the edge of the Yangtze River in Old Shanghai in China and a local man pointed out across the water and explained to me in uncertain English that that was where they were building an entirely new Shanghai of modern high-rises. And that they have. When I was there, westerners had just been allowed into the country for the first time. Many hotels didn't allow foreigners. If we stood in one place on the street for too long a large crowd would gather and stare because they'd never seen anything like us before. Often, someone would reach out and touch the blonde hair on my arm or my head.

Many things have changed over the years but one thing has stayed the same—the world is still both a beautiful and a painful place. In India, I saw a worker pulling an impossible load on a cart through the streets, his face showing both his struggle and his determination to survive. In a village on the island of Komodo, houses were built on tall stilts as protection from the dragons that had been known to come into the village at night to attack and drag off children, and yet the children played happily in the street there and greeted us with excitement. Aboard a ship to go scuba diving on the Great Barrier Reef, I felt so seasick I thought I would die and then moments later plunged below the surface into a glittering world of color and life.

Beauty requires pain and pain beauty. They cannot exist without each other, not in this world. We love people who die and shockingly disappear forever and then we love again. We suffer fear and discomfort to go where we have never been, to see something we've never seen.

Photographs make us feel like we are preserving this beauty or this pain, at least a reminder of it, keeping it for later. But even these images, like us, will eventually disappear.

There really is no other choice but acceptance.

Tree-lined canal in France

The Eiffel Tower

Houseboat on the Seine

Cairo train station

Cairo at dusk

Police — Cairo

Trash wagon — Cairo at night

Streets of Cairo

Streets of Cairo II

Streetcar and Mosque — Cairo

In the Valley of the Kings

Ferry across the Nile at Aswan

Woman in a field — Egypt

Luxor Temple — Aswan

Mosque — Cairo

Cairo

1. Awe

We stumbled out, before dawn, still a little stunned with sleep, into chill moist air, and started walking across the city to Sassoon Dock to watch fishing boats bring in the first catch, a few of us who'd met in the airport and shared a ride into the city and the same hotel, travelers.

The main streets of Bombay that early morning were still and quiet, little traffic. We passed high-rise office buildings and big, rich stores, a few just beginning to open here and there: shoes, electronics, books, pottery.

We cut over to the back alleys running parallel to the main boulevard and came upon an entire neighborhood of people asleep out in the open, in the dirt, on the walks, in the streets, on top of walls, under cars, wherever they could, lying scattered as if a bomb had gone off.

As we walked, some of them began to wake up. We tried to slip through, inconspicuous. Some men were naked, children barefoot. Women wore grimy sarees. Everyone was thin. A man knelt to wash himself under a faucet, another looked up from where he lay, dazed. Others rinsed their faces from puddles of water in the street.

We wound our way through the streets, people staring at us: a group of five westerners with small backpacks.

We'd made a simple plan—to walk the city and then go a day south to the palm-fringed, soft white sand beaches in the state of Goa and lie around there in the sun for a week or so before heading further into India.

Men and women began to work, to unload trucks, open storefronts, push wheelbarrows. A delivery truck pulled up in front of a small shop. The buildings were a series of shaky dilapidated tin sheds. Women folded their clothes and put them in neat little piles in select areas of the sidewalk.

All in tones of black, brown, grey.

We continued on, up to a beach, a huge plain of low tide muck that stunk like hell. A tiny woman came out of a nearby dingy tin shack, thin, ring in her nose, red dot on her forehead, saree, and in her arms, a skinny naked baby girl. The woman was laughing and pointing out to the beach, saying something in her language—until we finally understood that she was telling us not to go out there because it was their toilet and covered in human shit.

The dock was teeming, men running by in dhotis, barefoot, hurrying with baskets of fish on their shoulders, huge sacks of grain. A boss wearing trousers and a shirt yelled orders, and the bitter smell of rotten fish mixed with that of open sewers.

From a nearby quay, we stood and watched. Six or seven wooden trawlers rolled in the waves against a tall pier, each piled high with fish, and basket loads were tossed up one by one to men who then put them on their shoulders and shuffled off the dock in a long continuous line. Grey light filtered in from across the open bay and the Arabian Sea.

A crowd began to form around us, barefoot, wearing only dhotis, staring. Someone threw a fish at us from below.

Along one wall, a row of men and women, puffy-eyed from sleep, scrubbed their teeth with their fingers. A bar of brown soap was passed between them. One man hung his ass out over the edge and took a shit. Behind him, over his shoulder, we could see the fiery red sun as it rose above the sea and the feeling I had was: awe.

Sassoon Dock — Bombay, India

Our group at Joe Con's Cafe — Goa, India

India is shaped like an upright diamond, ancient, jagged-edged—an immense diamond: to the north are the highest mountains, to the west of them, arid desert; in the center high, cool foothills; in the south steaming thick jungle; and along either of the coasts ocean surf; all of it lush, teeming, extreme.

We decided to do a south to north arc, traveling fast, down from where we were along the west side into the pointed bottom of the diamond, and then back up to a place further north and into the Himalayas to Dal Lake.

Travel by boat

Men at the train station

Worker — New Delhi

Elephant in the street in Madras and Gary

Construction in Jaipur

Vegetable seller

Crowded train in the state of Kerala

Fishing village on the island of Fort Cochin

Child in the river — Madras

Kodaikanal Hill Station in Tamil Nadu

Taj Mahal — Agra, India

Girl selling drinks on the beach — Goa

Ox cart in Goa

Men on train

Houseboats on Dal Lake — Kashmir

Neighborhood on the lake

Houses — Dal Lake

Children in a boat on Dal Lake

Trucks en route from Kashmir

2. Driven over the Edge

It was a cold, grey day when we left Dal Lake in Kashmir, the surface of the water one long unbroken reflection. We took a bus south, our bags tied to the top, along the same road we'd come up. On either side, steep cliffs fell away out of sight. In the distance rose high, snow-topped mountains of the Himalaya. The bus jolted and the gears grinded. At some turns, our tires passed a foot away from the crumbling edge. I looked out the window to see a mangled wreck of a bus in the brush far below.

On the narrow two-lane road, we came up behind a truck and passed it. Then we came up behind another, and this time passed on a blind curve. When we were right up beside this second truck, our driver leaned out his window and yelled at the other man, not watching the bend in the road, the engine roaring. I had time to look up, see us in the oncoming lane of traffic and think—watch where the hell you're going.

And then, astonishingly, unbelievably, we drove straight off the edge of the cliff.

A woman screamed.

We sailed out into the air. I saw blue sky through the big front window of the bus. I came out of my seat, was floating free, feet first, looking out into that blue.

We seemed to hang there forever, unattached, open, now, now, now, now—

Then the bus tilted forward, and we fell.

People flew past me like the inside of a sweepstakes barrel. Things, bags, clothing sailed everywhere; screams, loud crashes.

We fell for what seemed like an incredibly long time. I had no idea what kind of cliff it was or how far a drop.

I thought, oddly, "I must land on my feet."

Then the bus slammed front first into the earth. When we hit, I felt a second of relief because it meant we'd finally reached the bottom. Then we began to roll.

The ceiling flew up at me, and I did land on my feet, and then it instantly gave way, as the bus turned over a second time, and I dropped headlong out of control back into the seats and was knocked out cold.

When I woke, I was standing, handing a woman out the door of the bus, down five or six feet to the ground, into someone's outstretched arms, a gouged-out open space where the door had been.

I was stunned to see I'd been moving around for I didn't know how long already, my body going on without my mind.

From below, I heard a voice and realized I was standing on top of a woman buried in debris, and she was looking up, calling, "Help me, help me." I bent down and dug her out of broken glass, twisted metal—an older Indian woman in a saree.

The bus swayed slightly, this way and that. I wanted to get off before we began to roll again. I jumped to the ground and turned to see that the bus had come to rest, actually, in the middle of a green field, next to a pink flowering tree, in a shallow valley surrounded by the high, snow-topped mountains, the road far above us, up on the cliff, winding off along a ridge in either direction. It was a beautiful place, the air crisp, clean, like a dreamy vision.

The top front of the bus was smashed in completely, the sides were bent, all the windows were gone, and the surrounding area was littered with debris. People were everywhere, moving about, lying down, limping away, crawling.

I looked up to see that we had fallen only briefly and then hit an incline and rolled the rest of the way.

A line of people mysteriously seemed to appear out of nowhere, stood along the edge of the road, looking down.

Our little group of now seven were stunned but ok.

"You okay?" I asked one of them, Hoss, an Australian.

"Fine. You?"

I took stock. There was a small pain in my leg, a dull ache, and some blood. "Yeah, I'm all right," I said.

In truth, I had never felt better in my life. Never more fully myself. Happier than hell: alive, full of energy, flying on adrenaline, talking a mile a minute, feeling glorious. Alive! I felt like singing. I kept saying to myself, we just went off the edge of a cliff in a bus.

We finally arrived at a hospital in the middle of the night. No one was on the streets of Jammu because of a week-long curfew to quell local rioting over we knew not what.

A trail of blood stains led up the front steps. A man in a white coat asked what we wanted.

We followed him to his office down a long dark hallway that smelled of alcohol and disinfectant, around corner after corner, and heard the echo of groans and occasional screams, which grew louder as we neared his office.

In the main hall a row of patients lay on the floor, one with a mangled limb, another bandaged, a few sleeping. Months later we would read that all three floors of this hospital had collapsed and hundreds of people were killed.

In his office, he looked us over briefly and then pronounced we were okay. The doctor began to make small talk. The room felt suffocating and I went back out, through the dark, echoing hallways to the front steps outside, where I could breathe again in the cool air and silence.

It was dark, no moon, only a dim light from the hospital. I felt filled with a sense of astonishment, even more so than what had become normal in those days.

As I sat, five men suddenly came out the front door carrying a stretcher with a dead body on it. They argued loudly in Hindi until one of them started shouting angrily, waving his free arm. Immediately, the others put the body down on the steps, yelling and gesturing back, so that it slanted diagonally, head first, making me wonder if it might slip off and go tumbling. Still arguing, they suddenly, surprisingly, went around the corner and disappeared.

For the longest time, I simply sat there alone with the corpse, its still, placid face staring up to the moonlight.

Nothing I could do.

Finally, all five of the men returned, talking among themselves. They each took a place around the stretcher, became quiet suddenly and then carried it off around the corner and into the night.

Following pages: landed in a field of green grass

3. The Dead are Everywhere

Hoss and I went into the guts of the city toward the river, down twisting narrow lanes, trudging along, stone walls rising up three stories on either side of us, every foot packed with people.

Varanasi, holy city, the City of Light, built on the holiest of rivers, the Ganges, where Hindus came to from all over.

It was hot. We climbed to the top of a deserted building, up a broken-down wooden staircase attached to its side. The structure creaked and shook. A piece broke off and fell to the dirt below.

We went past a broken window, green filth in a puddle on the floor inside. We startled a desperate, wire-thin dog crouched in the corner, its eyes too big for its head. It growled but lacked the will to get up.

We looked down to our left upon the wide, silt-thick river, to an astonishing sight: stone ramparts lined the shore and steep steps descended into the muck. These were the ghats. Thin, skeletal men and women moved about everywhere, dotting the landscape, wrapped in loose saris or dhotis, milling back and forth along the bank, throngs entering and exiting on streets that stretched out from the curved bank like spokes of a giant wheel, spokes that traveled out into the rest of India. Along these dirt streets: horse drawn carts, bicycles, scooters, huge horned oxen with satchels across their spines, a lone elephant, its owner clinging to its neck with his knees. A black English taxi with a human body tied precariously to its top, one arm dangling free, inched its way through the crowd and toward the shore. On the same street, a few meters behind it—another body, long black hair, partially enshrouded by a red saree and strapped to a wooden cart with no sides. The owner whipped the oxen and drove the cart lurchingly forward.

Everywhere below us was confusion and noise, naked bony limbs, black hair, bare feet, and always the dust in the air, rising as high as the three-story crumbling shack we were perched upon, always the smell of feces, human, animal—feces pressed to the sides of the buildings, cow pods in piles next to some of them, to be burned as fuel on open fires, and always the wet, dark, murky smell of the river. It drifted up to where we stood, and was the smell of mud, soot, filth, mixed with another odor so thick and everpresent that it permeated our jeans and t-shirts, our skin; stuck to our tongues and penetrated to the very follicles of our hair and through our pores, so that long after we'd showered the stench and taste and sight of it stayed with us. It was the smell of death, the smell of bodies being brought forward from the seething mass along the spokes of the wheel to the river's black, sooted, cement edge, to the ghats, where they were burned one by one on funeral pyres of logs and sticks ten feet high, to the sounds of festive, scratchy, religious music. A thin column of black smoke rose, and with it the acrid, gut-wrenching smell of burned flesh, until the entire city was permeated with it.

One man turned the charred white bones of each skeleton with a long pole and then scooped them up with a shovel
and carried them down to the river where he tossed them in at the edge, so that a pile was created, and the easy ripples of the tide carried a bit at a time out into the sacred river.

There were three pyres at this ghat, dusty mounds of charred remains and wood ash, thin columns of black smoke rising. The shrouded dead waited, in lines, at the feet of the living, on the hot cement, to be burned.

To die in Varanasi was to escape the wheel of karma, to escape your problems and ascend directly to Nirvana. To bathe or drink from the Ganges was to be cleansed of all your sins and renewed to the vigor of health. So from all over the country and the world, the rich came to die, the poor to beg from the rich, the scholars to study it all, the devout to be born anew, the lost to ponder, and the dead to have their ashes cast into the current.

All along the river's edge, people bathed, wading in slowly, pouring water over their heads, submerging themselves. Others prayed, meditated. In one place, women washed laundry by hand, rinsing each item, scrubbing it with a bar of soap, banging it on a stone again and again, and then laying it out flat to dry.
Out in the wide river, a large black barge moved slowly. It carried stacks of dead bodies of those who couldn't pay for wood and music and so were then taken out to the middle of the river, weighted, and dropped to the bottom.
Now and again a body slipped free, bobbed by.
We got lost on the way back in the labyrinthine alleys, so narrow we had to pass in single file, able to touch the stone walls on either side, which rose far above our heads. Locals looked at us in surprise as we passed, not used to seeing anyone like us in those parts of the city. On one wall, a rectangular cubbyhole was carved out of the stone and a man sat inside with a few papers and some pens and conducted some sort of business. In another, next to him, a woman sewed saris. In a shop window, behind glass, a bare wood plank shelf held only five pairs of yellowing dentures.
We followed the twisting, unmarked alleys for a long time, oblivious to where we were, forgetting the way back — on and on. Finally, we came out onto a street that seemed familiar, and slowly, we were able to find our way.

Bathing in the Ganges River — Varanasi, India

Varanasi on the Ganges River — India

Boats on the Ganges

Laundry

Getting a shave

Women cooking

The Ganges River — Varanasi

Woman walking along the Ganges River — Varanasi, India

Solitary boat on a beach in Goa

Praying man

Fisherman

Katmandu, Nepal

Flute sellers in Katmandu

Men in a doorway — Patna, Nepal

Market in Katmandu

Looking back across the valley, from where we had come,
as we hiked the Annapurna Trail in the Himalaya in Nepal

The beginning of the trail at Suikhet, Nepal

Women carrying slate on the Annapurna Trail

Village on the trail

Woman in a basket

Ghorepani. Altitude 9429 ft., the last lodging before Mt. Everest — Nepal

Ghorepani, Nepal

Annapurna

Sunlight on a hillside

4. Too Far

We went to the Patphong area, a red light district, where all the soldiers used to come for R & R back during the Vietnam War.

I was reluctant. I'd been to places like this before and I thought for sure we'd run into trouble. But Julie and Nicki were insistent. They wanted to see. I took only enough cash for the night, wore my high-top sneakers.

Bars with neon signs lined the street: the Pussy Galore. Eat Me Cafe. Rauncho Deluxe.

Guys on the street yelled out what the girls inside were doing, handed out little lists of their acts, Round-The-World, Bang the Drum, Tweak the Snake.

We agreed to have one round, bargained on the price with a guy at the door before going up a long set of stairs to a dark, smoky room on the second floor.

I'd seen my share of strip joints in the States but never what these girls were doing, using their parts to do tricks, blow whistles, shoot water pistols, pick up chopsticks. A Thai girl sitting next to us put her hand on my thigh.

When we got up to leave, our trouble began. They gave us a bill for ten times the amount of what we'd agreed upon.

We refused to pay it and, instead, left what we owed on the table and headed for the door.

Halfway there, however, a manager stopped us and slapped the money we had left into Tom's hand and said it wasn't enough. He then motioned and the front door was suddenly closed and a tough, wiry looking guy leaned against it with his arms folded over his chest.

"You pay first. All of it," the manager said. "Then you go out."

I felt closed in, held in place.

I thought, okay, here we go.

I got up into his face and he got into mine.

"Fuck you," I said.

I yelled whatever I could think of, just let it rip, to scare him, because I was scared, saying we'd tear the place to shreds, calling his mother a whore, telling him that I'd wrench his balls off and stuff them down his throat.

I watched it get to him, his face go pale. I saw it shock him. Americans, I could see him thinking.

All hell broke loose. There was a scuffling at the door as Gary tried to push his way out. People were screaming suddenly over the loud music.

A stripper came flying off the stage at me and landed on my head, her arm around my neck, scratching the hell out of my back. Instinctively, I shrugged her off, flinging her against the wall. But she stood up immediately and came charging right back. So I grabbed her by the arm and looked her in the face. "Stop," I said. "This does not concern you. This is between me and him." I don't know why I said it, but it seemed to calm her down and make her think twice. She stepped back and began screaming at me in Thai instead.

Julie and Nicki stood behind her a few steps, frozen in place.

The manager still blocked my path. He was tall for a Thai. "You want shit," I yelled at him. "You've got it, I'll never give in. We'll be at this for decades. You'll lose business."

He didn't get it at first, but we went back and forth like that for so long he finally believed me and he stepped back. He shook his head. "Okay," he said. "Pay only what you owe."

"Fine," I said. "Open the door first and let my friends go out. Then we'll pay."

"No," he said. "First pay."

"Like hell," I replied and began to yell at him again. I think he figured I was crazy. I might have been.

Finally, once again, he relented, not liking it very much.

He made a motion with his hand and the guy at the door stepped aside and it was opened, and everybody exited. Tom hung back a second, handed me the wad of money, "Don't give it to them until you are out," he said. When it was my turn, I stepped into the doorway and without counting it slapped the money into the manager's hand, the tough, wiry looking guy right next to him.

I was afraid to turn away, so I went down the stairs backwards, facing them.

As I went, my head slowly became level with the bottom of the door, until I was looking right into their feet, and then the manager, disgusted, stepped forward and aimed a front kick at my head.

What I had once learned, from taking martial arts a long time ago, came back suddenly, right then, when I needed it, and I moved just in time to the left. His kick missed, and I took a couple steps back up toward him, cursing.

Then the tough, wiry looking guy next to him stepped forward and threw a kick of his own. Again I dodged, and it missed my face by a fraction. But this guy made a mistake. He let his kick stay out there, not pulling it back in right away as he should have, and in those seconds, I reached up, instinctively, and caught his heel, surprising the hell out of both of us, but more so him. For a moment, I had him, teetering there by one foot.

I yanked, and he came flying down the steps on his back, his head banging, until he was laid out, and then I front kicked him myself hard in the crotch, two, three times and was going for it again, totally focused, not watching out, when, from my left, the manager returned, stepped up and connected with a full force kick to my face so hard that the pain exploded inside my head like hot knives. My nose broke. My blood went flying all over the place, over my legs, my arms, clogging my eyes, into my mouth, so that I couldn't see and could hardly breathe and I went into a kind of all out totally focused rage, committed to the very end, the whole of it coming out right then, the pain, the flux, the relentlessness, convinced in those seconds that I was going to die, a blind, automatic black emptiness. I ducked my head and leaned into the tough, wiry guy still down in front of me, protecting my face, so I couldn't be hit again, and pummeled him with both fists—to his balls, to his stomach, to his throat.

Chaos broke out all around me, people screaming, pushing, shoving, the steps jammed with too many, a riot breaking out.

I got my hands on his balls, the first time I'd ever felt a man's balls, and squeezed as hard as I could, until he began to scream a high-pitched endless whine and flew straight up into the air and onto his feet like magic and I stood up also and punched him flat-handed to the nose, and the crowd moaned, fell back a little, and I went for another and another, all the way now, fully in the blood-pumping fear of it, doing whatever I had to do.

It scares me to remember it now. I think I would have killed him if someone hadn't pulled me off.

But someone did. Suddenly there was an iron-like, vise grip around my stomach, so tight I couldn't exhale, and I was being yanked backwards, down the stairs.

I swung my elbows left and right, twirling, clearing out the crowd, trying to hit whoever had me, before they could drag me off into an alley and finish me off, but they were ducked too low.

Finally, at the bottom of the stairs, I began to make out a familiar voice over the din and then recognized it was one of my traveller friends, saying over and over again, "Pete, Pete, it's okay Pete. It's me. It's over. Stop," until I calmed and put it together.

We were standing in the street, surrounded by a huge crowd. I was covered in blood, my heart skipping. Inside, I was still up on the steps.

"It's okay Pete. It's okay."

"I want that son of a bitch," I yelled. I looked at the people gathered around me, "I want him now. I want that son of a bitch down here now. I want him arrested. I want his ass in jail."

From out of the crowd, a soldier appeared, an automatic weapon in his hands.

I yelled at the soldier what I wanted, but he was reluctant to do anything. Finally, he saw he had no choice.

"Come. Show me who," he said and began to lead me up the same stairs.

Gary stopped me. "Don't go back up there," he said.

I hesitated, and instead, amazingly, the manager suddenly appeared at the door, sticking his head out to see.

"Is that the man?" the soldier asked.

"That's him."

"You are sure."

"I'm sure."

The manager scowled at me.

"Okay. We go to station to fill out papers," the soldier said.

As we walked, I began to calm down a little. I felt the rage subside. I began to realize that I was going off into the back streets of Bangkok to who knew where, with an armed soldier, this manager, and a couple strippers who had come along, and I said to Gary, "Fuck this man. Let's just get out of here."

One of the strippers overheard, "What? What do you want?" she asked.

I looked at Gary, he at me.

"Money," he said suddenly. "Money? You want money?" she asked, latching onto the idea. "How much?" We looked at each other, did a quick calculation, and said an amount greater than what they had been trying to get from us in the bar.

They looked surprised. She said no.

"Then take his ass to jail," I said.

"Okay, okay." She spoke angrily at the manager in Thai, who then ran off like a bunny back to the bar and returned in a few seconds with a huge wad of bhat, which she slapped into my open palm.

"It is okay now?" the soldier asked.

"Yeah, yeah." I answered, and then seconds later all three of them were gone. We found ourselves alone standing in the middle of the street in the red light district of Bangkok with a wad of money in my hand, completely astonished, my clothes torn, bloody, nose aching.

We found the others at the end of the street and piled into a tuk-tuk. When I walked into our hotel, through the cafe, it caused a commotion. The owner came running to me, got an ice pack for my face.

I went up to the room, and in the shower down the hall, stripped off my clothes. Julie stood under the water with me. She rubbed the blood out of my shirt, my shorts, and then she slipped out of her own now wet clothes and stood close, carefully cleaning me up. I let the hot water sink into my scalp. I was still wired, still felt the blood rushing, still scared.

Only later did it really hit me, as I lay naked in bed under the slow turning fan, the sounds of rickshaws and voices outside on the street, Julie's hand on my arm, her soft even breathing. I thought, man, I've gone too far. I am out way too far.

Julie and the Taj Mahal — Agra, India

Koh Samui Island, Thailand

Sad man — Singapore

Ferry from Kowloon to Canton, China

5. Hog-Tied and Crazy

I entered China alone on a ferry from Kowloon to Canton. The ship touched dock just as the morning sky began to lighten. Up on deck, crewmen told us to wait to disembark, the custom agents still in bed. Looking down a long deserted street, in the eerie gray chill, I watched a column of green-clad soldiers goosestep past, on a cross street, guns on their shoulders, silent except for the click of their boots.

The great, vast Communist China, open to tourists for only five years at that point, before the coming capitalist boom, before new China. Full of rules, two different currencies, one for westerners, one for locals, towns we were not allowed to enter; people, hotels, places that had never seen a westerner before. We spoke no Chinese and few spoke English.

On a map, China is a huge jagged ink stain, a Rorschach blot, each region differing greatly from the others, open plain in the center, rugged mountains to the west and southwest, vast icy desert to the north, and a coastal plain along the east.

Train rides were hell. On one crammed-full train, a man tried to jump on board right in front of us as the train pulled out and people shoved him back. He hung from the door handles, his feet banging against the tracks until his screams caused somebody nearby to grab his arm and pull him up.

Inside that train, a seventeen-hour trip to Guiyang, everyone packed in body-to-body, the air smoky, the light dim. People cooked things on small burners in the seats, eating fish, spitting, farting, wiping babies butts, staring. When I inhaled, those around me pressed in against me so tightly I had trouble exhaling. In Cairo, I'd been caught in a riot on the street.

Panic had broken out and a man had jumped up on a bench and begun beating people over the head with a chair. I stood with my duffel between my feet. I felt the panic rise up in me.

I'd been told that the conductor at one end of the train would upgrade us, if we could find him, if there were seats. For forty-five minutes a traveler I'd met on the ferry and I squeezed through an endless sea of bodies, stepping on feet, hands, someone's head, falling against people, cursing, my duffel raised over my head, my arms aching. It was stupifyingly hot. I was covered in sweat.

Finally, we came to a small, bleak light, where a man sat at a tiny desk, people crowded all around shouting, waving money, the noise incredible from the roar of the train, the voices.

I pushed into the fray, wrote what I wanted in Chinese on a pad of paper, tracing the characters in the dark, from a little phrase book, the train rocking back and forth, then shoved the note into the man's face — first class seats.

Seeing we were foreigners, he asked an exorbitant price, and I hesitated.

"Just do it! Do it!" my companion yelled into my ear from behind, and I gave the man all the money we had.

We pushed through to a car beyond the conductor, slammed open the door and stepped into a completely empty dining car with two rows of perfectly set little tables each with cutlery, china cups, flowers in vases, not a soul there except for three waiters who stood off to the side in white tuxedos and black bow ties.

One of them took us to our room: two bunk beds with crisp white sheets, wool blankets, a china tea set, air-conditioning turned to ice cold. First class in a country with no classes.

Back in the dining car, we ordered drinks. At the far end, people pressed up against the glass door like fish in a far too small aquarium, their faces, legs, arms, flattened against the pane, their wide-open eyes staring in all directions.

In the car sat one other person, a Chinese man alone at a table with a cup of tea in front of him.

We remained for only a short time, sipping cold soda, feeling chilly in the air-conditioning; until a waiter finally came over and told us they were closing and we had to leave. We couldn't believe it. Why bother? All that space around us and so many people stuffed into the next car. It made us angry.

We stalled, and the lone Chinese man at the other table began to argue. Him they wanted to return to the cattle car.

We hung onto our seats for as long as we could, until the waiters stood over us, insistent, and we stood.

The lone Chinese man, however, still refused, shaking his head, saying something to them angrily.

The waiters left us and surrounded him, gesturing, shouting. The lone man yelled back.

Suddenly, they pounced on him like a pack of wolves and wrestled him to the floor. The man screamed, a high-pitched insane wail, and then lost it completely. He knocked his table over, and another, kicking the chairs left and right, howling and flailing, eyes wild, head back, drooling. But the three waiters were too strong for him, and they dragged him kicking and screaming down the center of the aisle toward the jam-packed car.

Brad and I just stood there at the opposite end, half-in and half-out of the exit, amazed and angry and shocked.

One of the waiters turned and yelled at us in Chinese, red-faced and enraged, dismissing us with a wave of his arm.

We backed out of the car.

Later that night when I went out to use the toilet at the end of the train car, I found the lone Chinese man there, completely out of his mind, hog-tied on the floor at the far end, his hands and feet roped together behind his back, his mouth gagged with a piece of cloth; struggling wildly, his eyes open wide, his screams muffled, foam at the corners of his mouth, gone.

   I backed away.

   He was still there in the morning when we got off to change trains.

Train station — China

Near the city of Yangshuo, China

Yangshuo County

Cable car over the Yangtze River in Chongquin, China

Ship in the fog — Yangtze River

Riverboat near Guilin

Barge passing through a neighborhood in Suzhou

Shipping

Chongquin

Ships on a river in China

Chongquin

Reading man in Beijing

Chickens in the market

Streets of China

Streets of Shanghai

Tianammen Square — Beijing, China

Along the Yangtze River

The Great Wall of China

The Great Wall of China

East across Indonesia

Boy on a horse cart

Heading to market

Tanning hides

Hiding boy

Sleeping in rickshaws

Island village — Indonesia

Komodo dragon

Village on Komodo Island

Colored volcanic lakes of Kelimutu — Flores Island, Indonesia

6. But the Earth is Round

From the airport I took a bus into Bondi Beach, where Hoss lived, and found his door and knocked on it. No one answered.

I walked down to the ocean, one block away.

Bondi had a beautiful stretch of brown-white sand and green surf, a small bay curving gently between two promontories, the avenue filled with cafes, fish shops, cheap hotels, bars. People strolled by in swimsuits, t-shirts, barefoot. Women sunbathed topless up and down the stretch of sand. Men wore small thongs. The streets were clean, orderly, paved, things new and modern. A breeze came in from the sea, over the white, strong surf. Everywhere everything was splashed with brilliant color, from the intense steady sun to the vivid clothes, pastel store fronts, new cars going by. It suddenly felt like I'd never really even seen color before: the flourescents, iridescent blues, reds, yellows.

Hoss and Nell had returned some months earlier to his home. When I returned to the apartment, they threw their arms around me. It seemed so long ago and another world away since we last saw each other in India.

They looked bright, healthy. Their condo was clean and close, a two-bedroom with den, and they quickly fixed up a room and invited me to stay for as long as I liked.

Gary was already there, in the den connected to my room. On the floor I recognized his pack and shoes. Since Singapore, he'd been here working in a factory. Tom was in Brisbane.

Nicki and Julie had found jobs and an apartment together in Balmain on the other side of town.

I lay in bed that night, sick and alone and confused, and wondered how long I could stay.

I tried to stop, to wait for change, to be with the friends I had there. I should have been able to. Everywhere I went was the smell of salt sea air and the sun. It was a beautiful, stunning, warm metropolis by the ocean. But it was too hard. I felt as if the world was waiting for me, just outside the city. The days became interminable.

I tried working a job in a warehouse on the edge of town, as an illegal, stacking shelf after shelf of goods, things I'd thought I'd left behind, things I remembered once wanting and needing but seeing no real value in anymore, stacks and stacks of them, little fuzzy things, deluxe models, replacement packs, add-ons, matching items, specials, sales. I walked the rows and rows, fifteen-feet high and fifty-yards long, wanting nothing, disgusted with myself, with all of it.

I quit and then got a job as a Removalist, a furniture mover, with a goofy guy who found his work out of the classifieds, relocating people from apartment to apartment, moving single refrigerators, dining room sets. He called me when he needed me, a couple times a week.

Some days we'd work late into the evening, hauling huge pieces of furniture down stairs, tying them onto the truck. On one job, I stood and looked out from the doorstep to the sea every few minutes.

In my free time, I went out of Hoss's apartment to the beach right there and walked, following paths that led around a series of rock cliffs to other beaches in small coves, attached to other neighborhoods, from Bondi to Tamarana, Bronte, Clovelly, Coogee.

For miles I could walk along the path and never leave sight of the ocean, people surfing on brilliant flourescent boards, laying nearly naked on towels.

I walked everywhere: Balmain, the Opera House, the park down by the water, the Bridge, Kings Cross, the Rocks, along the Harbour, took ferries across to Manly; moving, sweating, walking eight, ten hours a day.

Always I was jumpy, ready, expecting to move on to the next city any day.

Always I'd ask, in one way or another, even after I figured out not to ask anymore, "When do we leave? When do we move on?"

Eventually, I renewed my visa, my second, with no more available to me, deportation the penalty and no chance of ever returning if I got caught without one. It was a tourist visa which meant I was unable to work legally, no future to build there even if I knew what work that might be; my restlessness still unabated, my despair growing, my need for something ahead, I didn't know what, to finish the circle, perhaps, to move, still to just move, always to just move. I should have been able to stay in perfect Sydney and make a go of it somehow. That would be the normal thing, such a city like Sydney—but I couldn't. I just couldn't. After all of it, I still had not found my way.

After a month, I convinced Julie to travel Australia with me, though she was reluctant.

We went north by bus, through the center of the country, into Alice Springs and then up to Darwin and then east and back down along the Gold Coast. We visited opal mines in Coober Pedy. We hiked in the Outback and climbed Ayers Rock. Our bus broke down in the rainforest somewhere in Queensland, and we hitched a ride for a few hours to the next town with a cop or "copper" in a jeep who had to lock me in the cage in the back with a pile of booze he had just confiscated from some local Abbos because there wasn't enough room up front. We saw a sixteen-foot crocodile from a flat boat in Kakadu National Park. We walked huge vacant beaches in Queensland and eventually separated for three days while I went out on a boat to dive on the Great Barrier Reef.

It felt good to be back on the road and Australia was interesting and different, but for me, the travel felt too easy. Clean buses to quiet towns, no touts, no open sewers, everything recognizable, few risks, few surprises.

When we got back to Sydney, the hunger quickly consumed me again, the angst, the desire to move.

I felt both defeated and victorious. I didn't want to return but moving on suddenly meant moving back. I didn't want to go and I didn't want to stay.

But I had run out of room; moving across a sphere you eventually come back around. And I just had to go.

Bondi Beach — Sydney, Australia

Neighborhood on Bondi Beach — Australia

Kings Canyon in the Outback — Australia

Ayers Rock (Uluru)

North Western Queensland, Australia

Self-portrait — North Queensland, Australia

Mo'orea, Tahiti

7. Hear Monkeys Holler

I returned to my brother and his wife's family's farm, where they gave me a room to stay and I helped out in return, three hundred and eighty acres, the last remaining dairy farm inside of the Beltway that surrounded Washington D.C., in their family for the past three hundred and fifty years, given to them by the King, and due to be sold any year to city planners because of political pressure: a couple old houses, a couple barns, sheds, a chicken coop, fifty head of beef, fifty of dairy.

I slept on the floor in my room because the bed was too soft, but said nothing about it to my brother and his wife, kept my duffel partially packed, by the door.

Every once in awhile, I would panic, suddenly not knowing what to do with myself. A day seemed an incredibly long time to stay in one place.

I followed a truck in the fields in the wet summer heat, heaving heavy dusty bales of hay up onto the back, drenched, aching, tired in the first couple of minutes but continuing all day.

In the evening, we ate plates heaped with steak, potatoes, bread with thick pats of butter. Me, my brother, his wife, her brother, their parents, sisters, in-laws, cousins coming and going.

We had a view from the porch out over the fields in one direction and in another, hills that rose up like shoulders, an old broken-down barn at the top, a ravine cutting its way through the center of the property.

I thought of walking South America, from the north to the southern tip of Patagonia.

I lay awake, often, unable to sleep, and just outside, in the cool of the quiet night, I could hear monkeys holler.

I took the canvas cover off my old car, a nineteen sixty-six Chrysler Newport convertible, long, bright red wings flaring in the back, white top, a pair of yellow die hanging from the mirror.

In the winter, it had been buried completely in snow drifts. Inside, its floorboards were rotted through. They cracked when I stepped in, and the white top ripped and blew away in dust as I helped it open slowly and tuck itself back into its place, never to be put up again, decayed to nothing, though the engine started right up.

I drove into D.C., speeding out along route 50 and 295 to the Capital Street Bridge, past the Stadium, Stanton Park, the Hill, the Capitol Building, down to the Mall area with the Washington Monument, reflecting pool, Lincoln Memorial, White House, the city I was born in. I drove back around to my father's house two blocks off the Mall, where I stopped out front and sat looking at the door where he once had been, sold now, unable to enter like I always had, the overhanging shade trees there, sound of traffic nearby, my engine running.

It was the shock of death that affected me the most, the sudden finality, not the missing of them. How inexorably everything goes right on.

I drove out New York Avenue back to 50 and then south down 301 to 4, into Waldorf, to a storage lot, punching in a series of numbers from a packet of info I'd kept in my duffel all this time. A huge metal gate rolled aside and I slowly eased down the first row, finding it by feel, before then checking the numbers in the upper right corner to make sure I had the right one.

I slipped the key into the bin's padlock and rolled the flexible door up into the ceiling, smelling dust and dampness as shafts of sun spilled into the wide, rectangular cement space filled to bursting with boxes, furniture, small appliances, clothing, odds and ends.

It was all still there, just as I had stacked it before going, two years ago.

Scraps of memories. Most of it my father's stuff. A huge old round oak dining table with matching chairs, two big cherry bookshelves with ornate corners, old paintings in thick carved frames, stacks of fine wood end tables, a lawnmower, lamps, two couches, an easy chair, boxes stuffed with old papers, records, letters, momentos, photographs, books, all piled six-feet deep to the ceiling.

The sun beat down and heated the cement and tin storage bin and the pavement around it and my red convertible.

I began to sift through it all, taking what I could in the back of the huge car, stuffing odds and ends and boxes in the wide back seat and into the massive trunk, until I was sweating and thirsty.

In the next few days I came back again and again and slowly emptied the bin out, spreading the stuff everywhere, to other people's houses, basements, secondhand stores, anyone who would take it, my sisters, brother. I didn't want any of it anymore, wanted it out of my life and away from me.

I wasn't afraid of dying. It was the giving up of things that was so painful, that was slowing me down. I had to let it all go, let it go.

On the last load, I slid the flexible bin door down, latched it, slammed the heavy door of my car and pulled out onto the street. The wind blew in my face, the sun hot, constant, the car big enough to house a family in some places I'd been, flying down the highway.

It's a paradox: the impermanence of things, and the desire to have.

On the farm, dogs from the nearby city neighborhoods often roamed the fields, and every now and then took up living in the ravine that cut across the property, a small stream at the bottom of it, thick foliage and high trees growing in and around it, the dogs eating whatever they could find, quail, rabbits, frogs, rotting plants, never going back to being pets again.

As long as they stayed out of our way, we didn't bother with them, but, eventually, they started foraging for more, like they did that summer, and we each would carry a shotgun with us when we went out walking.

One evening two of them came up onto the back porch and ripped open the garbage and spilled a sack of barley. Another time, as my brother's wife's father, Tom, came around a thick, vegetated corner, one of the dogs, a big, bright yellow mutt stepped out of the bush and bared its teeth and growled, advancing toward him slowly.

From the screened-in porch, we once watched the same yellow dog, in the company of another darker brown one, break from the tall corn field and go after a two-day old calf, bringing it down and going for its throat before my brother could get on the three-wheeler and race across the bumpy fields to the other side of the ravine and chase it off.

On a hot afternoon one day, I took a shotgun from the corner near the door where we left them and followed the dirt track down across the ravine. On all sides the corn was higher than me, rustling in the wind, and I climbed to the top of the tallest hill, to the old worn-out barn there.

It was rickety and weathered, smelled of sun-heated wood, grey, splintering. Inside, the roof rose to a startling height and it was cool and shady and smelled of old hay and cow manure. Pigeons fluttered far above among the thick, long, wood beams, a moist, hushed cathedral of quiet.

I sat out front in the sun on an old log, and from there could look out across the entire farm, to the highway that circled the land, the sound of traffic a constant insect whirring, the sky a clear, turquoise blue, a few puffy white clouds. In the far distance, the very top of the pencil-shaped Washington Monument downtown peaked above the horizon.

I was sweating. I liked to walk and walk, the shotgun over one arm, the grasses and corn up to my waist, over my head.

Once in awhile I shot a shell off, just to hear its sound, to feel the powerful kick of the explosion in my arms, shoulder.

How incredible that none of the physical things we touch, stay, but fall away always.

On this day, I sat until everything stilled, my heart, my breathing, the spinning earth itself.

A cool breeze came up from the ravine far off and below to my right, where I could see the farmhouse, my bright red topless convertible, the other barn and buildings, the pond, a few head of stark black cattle nearby.

I could see my father standing there, so real was he to me, and my mother, as she left the room and turned off the light. I could smell the sea off Bali, see the white, majestic peaks of Nepal, feel the heat beat down in the outback.

Pete Hendley is a photographer and writer. He has traveled extensively and lived in Australia, Guatemala and Mexico. He is the 2019 Single Image Spotlight Winner for Travel photography in *Black and White Magazine* and the author of *LCI 85: The Military Career of Lt(jg) Coit Hendley Jr. During the Invasions of North Africa, Italy, and Omaha Beach on D-Day: His Papers and Photos,* and the travel guide *Hiking The Grand Canyon: The South Kaibab and Bright Angel Trails; Photos and Tips.* He has published photographs with *The Travel Channel, Travel & Leisure, USA Today, Forbes, Detroit Free Press, The Cut, Virtuoso* and more and is a stock photographer for Getty Images and Alamy. He has also published in *Cricket Magazine; Aethlon: The Journal Of Sport Literature;* and *The Workshop.* He is a graduate of The University of Iowa Writers' Workshop and makes his home in Iowa City, Iowa.

Made in the USA
Middletown, DE
24 February 2021